FOR YOUR GARDEN

Pools, Ponds, and Waterways

FOR YOUR GARDEN

Pools, Ponds, and Waterways

DAWN TUCKER GRINSTAIN

Grove Weidenfeld
New York

A FRIEDMAN GROUP BOOK

Copyright © 1992 by Michael Friedman Publishing Group, Inc.

Published in the United States by
Grove Weidenfeld
A Division of Grove Press, Inc.
841 Broadway
New York, New York 10003-4793

Library of Congress Cataloging-in-Publication Data
Grinstain, Dawn Tucker.
    Pools, ponds, and waterways / Dawn Tucker Grinstain. — 1st ed.
        p. cm.
    Includes bibliographical references.
    ISBN 0-8021-1407-5 (alk. paper)
    1. Water in landscape architecture.   2. Gardens—Design.   3. Water
gardens.   4. Aquatic plants.   I. Title.
    SB475.8.G75   1991
    714—dc20   91-12274
                                                                              CIP

POOLS, PONDS, AND WATERWAYS
was prepared and produced by
Michael Friedman Publishing Group, Inc.
15 West 26th Street
New York, New York 10010

Editor: Sharon Kalman
Text Editor: Karen Spinks Stearns
Art Director: Jeff Batzli
Designer: Susan Livingston
Photo Editor: Anne K. Price

Typeset by Bookworks Plus
Color separation by United South Sea Graphic Art Co., Ltd.
Printed and bound in Hong Kong by Leefung-Asco Printers, Ltd.

First Edition 1992
10 9 8 7 6 5 4 3 2 1

Dedication

To my loving husband Stuart for encouraging me to
accept challenges; and to my understanding
son Aaron for providing an abundance of
smiles and hugs.

Acknowledgments

I would like to thank the following people who helped
me write this book: Gordon Kurtis, who helped with the
research; Karen Stearns, who line-edited the book,
Rosalyn Layton, who typed the manuscript, and
Sharon Kalman, for her patience.

Table of Contents

Introduction

Acool pond sparkles in the sunlight, a large goldfish swims slowly by, leaving a tiny ripple in its wake. The pond is surrounded by lush foliage, the gentle perfume of jasmine is in the air; all is right with the world.

There is something mysterious about water. We are, by instinct, drawn to it. We find extreme beauty in it. We are comforted by the sound of it. We are sustained by drinking it, and we are calmed by being near it. Few can explain why.

Making water a part of your landscape can add a wonderful dimension to the beauty of your garden. And there are so many affordable ways to do it. Not only can a water feature increase your property value, but the aesthetic and functional qualities will be very rewarding as well.

Just as the architecture and interior design of a home should intertwine, so should the landscape design incorporate the qualities of both the existing environment and the desired environment, creating a haven of beauty and tranquility.

A pool, pond, or waterway can be an integral part of any design concept, whether the outdoor space is large or small, flat or contoured. Your water feature, placed within the appropriate setting and surrounded by site-enhancing plants, will prove to be an ever-changing source of fascination.

A water feature may also be functional—a swimming pool for exercise, a spa for therapeutic use, a fountain to overshadow the noise of nearby traffic, a reservoir to retain water and attract wildlife. These and many other uses can be incorporated into the design of your pool, pond, or waterway in forms that truly enhance your garden.

A setting of tranquility is created by balancing natural and man-made components.

© Balthazar Korab

Where does one look for design ideas? A glimpse at the history of water in the landscape is a good place to start, providing wonderful examples to guide you in your selection and design process.

Pools, Ponds, and Waterways in History

The use of water in the landscape first appeared in history as both religious and functional. In ancient Egyptian tomb paintings of the temple garden at Thebes, a walled garden was depicted as located

adjacent to a canal, providing access to water. The plants that were used in the water garden—lotus and papyrus—also provided inspiration for the architectural detail found in the columns, walls, and floors of the garden.

The Islamic influence of the fourteenth, fifteenth, and sixteenth centuries provides us with wonderful examples of how water was used for functional and aesthetic purposes in areas where it was of limited supply.

Left: *Reflecting pools and narrow channels of moving water, such as those seen at the Alhambra in Spain, enhance the architecture of your home and create a cooling effect when summers are warm and dry.*
Above: *A pond of still water becomes one of movement and animation when fish are incorporated into the feature.*

Above: *The balance, proportion, and placement of elements in the garden creates an environment appearing to be made by nature.* Opposite page, left: *The presence of a water moat within the Forbidden City in China contributes to the serenity of the setting.* Opposite page, right: *In this beautiful setting in Nanking, China, the geometrical lines of the pool and the architecture are contrasted by the presence of water lilies.*

One perfect example is the Court of the Oranges in Cordova, Spain, where water is stored in a rectangular pool, and is channeled into an irrigation system where it is used to water citrus trees. The area is enclosed by walls and other structures that create a beautifully shaded and fragrant courtyard.

At the Alhambra in Granada, Spain, the Moorish architecture is enhanced by beautiful reflecting pools adjacent to jets of water and channels within the courtyards. The terraced gardens of the nearby Generalife, the summer retreat of the kings of Granada, are quite fascinating with their waterways that maneuver from one pool to another, jets splashing and creating a natural music. In a region where water is a precious commodity, these pools, ponds, and waterways add an aesthetic quality to the environment.

The ruins of Pompeii reveal that Roman homes were organized around a central courtyard or atrium that provided a mingling of indoor and outdoor spaces. The roof over the atrium was open directly over a pool where rain water could collect. Water for pools, fountains, and jets was piped in to create courtyard gardens with blooming and fragrant plants. They also served as water features for both aesthetic and functional purposes.

The Chinese and Japanese cultures developed the Oriental garden, where water is prevalent as an element of the design. The water may be reflecting and tranquil or moving with energy and sound. Oriental gardens imitate nature and often use water to represent a lake, river, or ocean. Every bridge, lantern,

rock, and plant in the design has a symbolic meaning, which transforms the garden into a true work of art. These gardens portray a respect for nature, and offer a setting that is subtle and relaxing.

Water is such an essential part of the Oriental garden that, in areas where water is scarce, the Japanese developed dry rock gardens. Water is not used in these gardens, but is represented by large rocks, stone, gravel, and sand. The placement of these elements is carefully designed to symbolize land forms and the flow or ripple of water.

Medieval European monasteries developed the cloister garden with influences from Roman and Persian predecessors. The garden was divided into quadrants by intersecting paths. The focal point of the garden was a water feature, used for religious purposes, drinking, watering, or bathing.

With influences from Middle Eastern traditions from the twelfth to the fourteenth century, the cloister garden was refined into the "paradise garden," the water pond still a vital resource of the home. It was further complemented with ornamental fountains laid out in formal curvilinear or geometric designs.

The ornate designs of the Renaissance period extended the architecture into the landscape through the organization of spaces on a central axis. In gardens as elaborate as these, focal points often included elaborate water features.

Northwind Picture Archives

The Renaissance period of the fifteenth and sixteenth centuries was a period of scientific study and elaborate works of art. Water features were developed with unusual effects and rich detail. In regions such as Italy, where water was readily available, gardens were situated on hillsides and water was manipulated from rivers and streams. The natural water pressure created by gravity carried the water through a series of waterfalls, pools, and ornate fountains.

In the terraced gardens of Villa Lante, at Bagnaia, water is the central axis, cascading through troughs, canals, and fountains to settle into pools set in a symmetrical plan.

The Villa d'Este at Tivoli is a magnificent example of the use of hydraulics with countless water features, including the famous water organ. Air was hydraulically forced through organ pipes and streams of water struck the organ keyboard, producing unusual sound effects such as singing birds, cannons, and tunes played through the organ pipes. The

advancement of science and the arts during the Renaissance period brought together a unification of architecture and geometry with the natural landscape, all through the use of water.

The designs of French gardens were greatly influenced by the Italian Renaissance period. Like the Italian designs,

The intricate patterns created in French gardens offered ornate compositions that used water as the focal point. These gardens provided a strong contrast to the adjacent countryside.

French gardens were thought to be a reflection of their owners' affluence and social or political importance. This period is considered by many as the high point of garden history and tradition. Gardens were not only an extension of the architecture, but could expand beyond the geometrical, ornate design and continue into the countryside.

At the Palace of Versailles grand vistas are highlighted by fountains with sculptures that reflect into the large pools.

A perfect example of the grand French design and its use of water is the palace at Versailles, outside Paris. Water was used in ornate fountains that also served as sculptural focal points when the water was not operating. Large pools dramatized the expanse of the property and reflected the many sculptures and adjacent dense growths of trees. When viewing the grounds from the palace or from one area to another, one can appreciate the detailed composition and progression of the architecture, elaborate water gardens, and the distant natural landscape.

The seventeenth and eighteenth centuries brought forth the Romantic landscape garden of the English countryside. Its influence was derived from the theories of Romantic literature and paintings. The philosophy was that ''all nature is a garden and the most appropriate design for a garden is one that appears as if it had always been there." Formal gardens of the past were torn out and replaced with free-form lakes, streams, and valleys, which were framed by groupings of trees to create picturesque landscapes. Chatsworth in Derbyshire was one such classic garden. Here, famous water features from earlier seventeenth-century formal water gardens are blended into a natural pictorial composition.

The nineteenth century in America brought about a philosophy in landscape design influenced by the writings of Andrew Jackson Downing (1815-1852) in "Treatise on the Theory & Practise of Landscape Gardening." He proposed that landscape design should complement the architecture of a home; meaning that landscape should have an overall unity, brought together by a variety of elements—water, structures, plants, sculptures—to carry out a single design.

So many gardeners and designers have used water as an element in landscape design, and in so many ways. Whether set in a grandiose scale or in an intimate garden, similar design principles can be applied. Innovative, classic, and contemporary design concepts for the use of water in the landscape can all be transposed, and are applicable to any situation. By studying famous gardens, we can obtain wonderful ideas and inspiration to guide and influence us through our own design process.

In the following chapters you will find photographs, illustrations, and information pertaining to many of the aspects involved in creating and maintaining water features. I am certain that you will find these wonders as fascinating and beautiful as I do. I have seen many of the wonderful gardens mentioned in this book, and they are even more breathtaking in reality than in pictures.

So, whether you seek information and ideas for an upcoming project, or you just like to dream, the following chapters will provide you with valuable and inspiring information.

chapter one

Options to Choose From

*I*ncluding water as part of the landscape is possible in any garden. It is only necessary that the design suit you, the setting, and the purpose for which it is intended.

The form in which the water is presented helps to create the mood of the setting. It will transpose the garden into an environment that is placid, dignified, playful, or droll. Water will give the garden life.

A still pond provides visual variety as the reflections change with the time of day and movement of the wind.

© Derek Fell

Water can be presented in the garden in many different forms. Your first decision in selecting the type of water feature for your garden should be whether the water in your landscape is to be still or moving.

Pools and Ponds

Pools and ponds of still water provide reflective qualities that enhance the beauty of the garden. As the light changes and the clouds move, shadows and colors in the landscape multiply and are mirrored in the water. An ornamental reflecting pool need not be large. Something as simple as an old stone trough can provide a lovely display of reflecting light. An improvised pond made from a wooden barrel, sunk in the ground and planted with a beautiful miniature water lily can be attractive and unusual. A small square pool can create a mirror effect for the reflection of a waterside bonsai tree. A reflecting pool as part of a sculpture garden adds another dimension to the artwork.

© Derek Fell

Swimming pools can provide a wonder-ful, reflective beauty to the garden as well as be used for recreational activities. A pool for swimming laps does not have to be as wide or as deep as a typical swim-ming pool. Jacuzzis and hot tubs can pro-vide therapeutic use and serve as reflective pools when not in use. Painting the surface of any pool or pond with dark colors will increase its reflective quality.

Providing wide steps into a pool extends the paving into the water, inviting people to sit, refresh, and enjoy.

© Charles Mann

Above: *This formal pool is softened by a border of plantings both within, cascading over, and surrounding the feature. Notice how the vertical form of the irises contrasts to the round form of the pool.* Opposite page: *The strong horizontal lines of this channel of water are enhanced by the presence of water lilies and a border of colorful plants.*

Still water is also appropriate in natural and informal settings. The plants may be immersed, growing in and out of the water, and fish may be living in the pond, creating a dimension below the surface.

Formal and geometrical lines may be appropriate with the architecture of a home, yet a more natural setting may be desired for the garden. The incorporation of natural materials such as boulders, a wood deck, and cascading plants will soften the edges of a formal-shaped pool or pond, creating a fusion between formality and nature.

With careful planning and construction, ornamental pools and ponds may be linked with swimming pools to create an extended water effect. The sensitive placement of lush water plants, bridges, or decks can provide a physical separation. However, visually the water features appear to be a single element. Ornamental pools and ponds can also be integrated around a swimming pool to soften the typically hard, formal edges.

A shallow bowl, basin, or birdbath can serve as a reflecting pool. The benefit of their small size is that they are portable and can be moved as you please. These features can be very interesting additions to the garden, especially when placed near a seating area or along a walkway to be viewed nearby.

Waterways

Pools and ponds become visions of variety, vitality, and constant change when enhanced with moving water. The spar-

© Nancy Hill

kling qualities of the water add fascination to any feature, and the soothing sound muffles the noises of modern-day life. The feeling of water from a fountain running through your hands, the splash from a waterfall, or a drink from a spring is soothing and refreshing. Moving water can bring life and variety to an otherwise static environment.

The forms of moving water are endless. Waterways are, by definition, navigable bodies of water. Nature shows us perfect examples of waterways through babbling brooks, streams, and waterfalls. Through winding courses, irregular placement of pebbles, rocks, mossy boulders, and wild moisture-loving plants, waterways create a natural setting. You can recreate this environment in your garden without having a feature that is large, wide, deep, or elaborate. Rather, a steady source of water, and the positioning of solid objects (such as boulders) to change the pace and direction of the water's flow will provide the visual interest so attractive in a natural waterway.

© Charles Mann

Below: *A site that contains grade changes, a backdrop of foliage, and natural rock outcroppings is a great location for a naturalistic pond and waterfall.* Right: *Few can resist crossing a pond when pavers extend from one side to another.*

The ability to cross moving water is a wonderful garden experience. Placing stepping stones, extended pavers, or a bridge over the water brings more interest and enjoyment, enabling the viewer to enjoy the garden from different angles. It also makes more of the garden accessible and useful because additional spaces and surprises can be added.

© Derek Fell

Water can navigate through canallike channels and many include a series of cascades or weirs (a notch through which water flows). This type of water effect is suited for a more formal setting where a naturalistic stream would seem out of place. A channel, as well as a natural stream, is set on an extended line and creates an axis from which the surrounding garden should be developed.

Waterfalls

Waterfalls add excitement to the feature and there are numerous ways to create them. The *Sakuteiki,* written in eleventh-century Japan, established strict rules for garden design. In discussing the movement of water, ten different forms of waterfalls were listed, including: linen falling, thread falling, uneven falling, glide falling, and straight falling. In today's terms these might also be described as informal weir, trickle fall, stepped falls, formal curtain fall, and overhanging fall.

Whether the water falls swiftly onto rocks, creating a mist and a roar in the air, or is simply a single spout trickling into a pool, the movement and sound of the moving water will always catch people's attention.

Fountains

Fountains bring a mood of celebration, a festival of light and water. Incorporating a fountain into the garden sets a definite focal point as one of its most ornamental features. The word "ornamental" does not necessarily mean that a fountain should be carved of stone with great

© Derek Fell

detail or that dolphin-carrying cupids spray water into another body of water. The fact is that the simpler the detail, the more successful the design. The fountain must work within the context and character of the surrounding garden.

Sound, energy, and continued vitality will be added to your pond when you include a fountain of dynamic water.

A simple water fountain provides beauty and sound, and it is easy to install. Surrounding your water feature with plants integrates it into the setting.

A single jet of water from a wall fountain can provide the rich, clear sound and sparkle that is attractive and enticing. The splashing water and glistening of light created by a tiered fountain provides energy and music to any outdoor foyer, atrium, or courtyard.

Water features, such as fountains, must be able to stand on their own aesthetically throughout the colder months when water is not available due to freezing. A grand example of this is the Apollo Fountain in the gardens of the Palace of Versailles. However, a site this large is quite unusual and a water feature this size is not generally warranted or desired. On a reduced scale and setting, however, the effect and purpose of the water feature should be similar.

The fountain should not only be a water source, but a piece of art as well, as is seen in Japanese gardens. A traditional feature, such as a stone basin with water streaming out of a bamboo spout, can stand alone or play a part in an entire garden setting.

Dry Water Rock Gardens

The Japanese developed the dry rock garden for areas where water was not readily available. The rocks, gravel, and sand were carefully placed and formed to represent vast oceans, mountain lakes, or ripples in a pond. If a Japanese garden fits within the context of the architecture and interior design of your home, then it is appropriate to carry this design theme into the garden.

If this is not the case, then the principles of Japanese design may still be applied to your garden, but into different styles and settings. Water basins and pools may be imitated by placement of rock and pebbles. Wild grasses, lilies, and irises may be planted along the edge to further enhance the setting. A natural drainage swale (a low-lying or depressed, and often wet, stretch of land) existing or needed in the garden is a perfect opportunity for a dry stream bed. The naturalistic placement of boulders, stone, and sand with stream-type plantings will create a surprising, disguised dry water garden.

This rock garden provides the mood of a stream without the presence of water. The Japanese maple cascading over the rocks adds to the river bank setting.

© Derek Fell

Bog Gardens and Wetlands

A natural bog garden or wetland is a low-lying spot in the natural terrain where water sheds from higher ground or where the water table beneath the soil is high, creating a riparian (water loving) environment. The innermost area of the garden, also the lowest in elevation (even if only slightly), may contain aquatic life. Reeds, rushes, ferns, and irises create a pondlike appeal. As the level of soil rises from the waterlogged area, riparian vegetation exists. Moisture-loving shrubs may spring up from the surrounding grasses and meadow-type plantings.

A bog garden or wetland can be artificially created in low spots of the garden that have poor drainage or are continually wet. The benefit of a bog garden is that it is simple to create, requiring only dirt, water, and plants. A bog garden may also be created in a tub of any material, such as wood, ceramic, or stone. (It also should have a drain plug for ready drainage.)

Using water-loving plants in a bog garden provides a pondlike setting without the installation expense and maintenance of a water feature.

A bog garden provides the opportunity to have water-loving plants and even wildlife in the garden without the necessary expense and installation of a pool, pond, or waterway. A bog garden may serve as a focal point in the landscape or it

© Derek Fell

Working With a Landscape Architect or Garden Designer

Working with a professional landscape architect or garden designer is time well spent, especially when dealing with large projects such as a pool or waterway. Consultation with a professional will aid you in the design of your garden and water feature. The best way to select a consultant is by obtaining referrals from others who have used his or her services. If no such referral can be obtained in this way, contact the American Society of Landscape Architects (A.S.L.A.) for professionals in your area.

Contact the landscape architect or garden designer and invite them to your home for an interview and consultation. Preview their portfolio, which should consist of drawings and photographs of residential gardens they have designed. Visit some of the projects they have already completed if you can. Communi-

may be the transitional area between a natural pool or pond and another area of the garden. A wide variety of waterside plants provides beauty and interest in the garden, creating the cool, soft pleasures of a wild water-garden atmosphere.

cate to the consultant the elements, materials, plants, and colors you would like to have in your garden. Feel free to indicate those items that you don't want. Select a consultant who has created environments that you like, whose personality you enjoy, and with whom you can speak freely.

Form a contractual agreement with the consultant. Based upon your desires, they will then begin to compose a landscape that is appropriate to your setting and works within your budget. They will communicate their ideas through the development of sketches and drawings. Based upon meetings with you, the design will be revised and refined from preliminary drawings through final working drawings, which will be used by those installing the project.

Following is an explanation of many of the materials available for use in water gardens.

This beautiful pool is evidence that working with a professional to create your water environment can help develop your property in ways you may have never dreamed.

© Balthazar Korab

Materials

Whether you choose to work with a landscape architect or garden designer, or decide to install a water feature yourself, there are many methods of affordable installation for water in the garden. Your chosen feature may be as complex as a formal custom-made pool or as simple as a small cast-stone bowl.

In general, there are three types of water accents: traditional pools with straight walls and geometric designs; natural, informal pools or ponds with curvilinear lines and sloping sides; and prefabricated bowls and basins. Each feature may be constructed with alternative materials and methods. Complexity of the design, existing site conditions, and your budget will be the primary factors in determining which materials to select.

No matter what materials you choose, they must be durable, watertight, strong, and resistant to weathering and cracking. A well-thought-out design, the use of quality materials, and proper methods of installation and construction will produce a successful water feature that will be easy to maintain and will last a long time.

Pool liners are a very popular and relatively inexpensive method of pool construction. A pool liner consists of a sheet of heavy-gauge polyethylene plastic or rubber material. The most durable are polyvinyl chloride (PVC), reinforced PVC, and rubber (with a terylene web). The sheet is placed in the excavated area (allowing sufficient overlap of material for ledges and to secure the liner) and shaped by the weight of the water as it is filled. Make sure there are no sharp objects or stones under the liner that could cause damage. A layer of sand may be placed beneath the liner to provide a firm protective base.

Anchor the liner by tucking it into the soil with a metal strip or by weighing it with heavy stones. The edging should be camouflaged with plants or boulders.

Plastic or fiberglass preshaped pools and ponds have made it easier to add water features to a garden. They are an

The combined use of brick and tile integrates the pool with the jacuzzi. The splash of water creates a natural music and offers fun to those sitting beneath its fall.

excellent alternative to concrete, especially where weight might be a critical factor. Less expensive plastic pools are vacuum molded in a tough, weather-resistant plastic. They are easily transported and accessible to most sites. Their flexibility, however, can make installation difficult.

Compared to plastic, fiberglass is rigid, freestanding, and the easiest to install. Fiberglass pools are very durable and can easily be made permanent features in the garden. To install, place the pool in an excavated hole of the same shape, but slightly larger. The pool should be set level on a sand base for stability. Be certain there are no sharp objects or stones in the sand. Refill the hole with rock-free material excavated for the pool as you fill the pool with water to maintain stability.

Concrete is perhaps the best and most commonly used material for constructing pools, ponds, and waterways. It can be formed and finished in a wide range of shapes and colors. As long as the concrete is mixed and handled properly, the pool

will be low in absorption (watertight), resistant to freeze–thaw cycles, durable, and crack resistant. For most pool work, it is recommended that three-thousand-pound (1.6 t) material be specified at least six inches (15 cm) thick, with reinforcement of wire netting or steel bars, depending upon the size and type of the structure. Finally, the pool should be treated with a waterproofing agent to ensure it will not leak.

Concrete contains a substantial amount of lime, which is harmful to both fish and aquatic plants. The pool must be cured to eliminate any harmful substances. When the concrete is dry, fill the pool and empty it at least two times within a ten-day period to flush out the lime. A neutralizing agent applied once the concrete is dry should eliminate any chance of trouble.

The color of the surface of the pool material will affect the appearance of the water. Light, reflective colors will make the water appear clear and transparent. Dark colors cause the water surface to be reflective. In most situations, the dark color is preferred. Dark colors also help to camouflage any equipment in the pool.

Swimming pools require more sophisticated design and construction considerations than smaller pools, ponds, and waterways. Because of the excavation, and electrical and mechanical considerations, the structural design and construction of a swimming pool should be done by competent engineers and contractors.

border materials

The border of your water feature is the area between the water and the surrounding planting areas or paving. There are many different materials that can be used for the border or edge treatments of your pool, pond, or waterway. The materials used will reinforce the style of the feature and define its form.

© Charles Mann

This man-made waterfall appears very naturalistic due to the meandering course and sensitive treatment of the border, consisting of rock and lovely plantings.

Formal pools and channels are typically geometrical in form. Therefore, the border treatment may be of formed or precast concrete, masonry-cut stone, brick, tile, or even an overlapping wood deck (hiding a concrete coping). A paving material adjacent to the pool may extend to the water's edge, creating the border. Boulders may be used on the pool's edge, but this requires creative planning to maintain the integrity of the formal design.

Informal pools and ponds are typically freeform in shape with curvilinear lines. The materials used for bordering may be a bull-nosed brick, to add a more formal appearance, thereby easing the transition between the formal architecture of the house. Rougher, more natural materials such as stone, boulders, or broken concrete may also be used. The quantity of rock used should depend upon the style of the existing setting. If the landscape is already rock-strewn, further rock ornamentation will complement the design.

To make the border appear established and naturalistic, a minimum of one third

© Derek Fell

of it should be set below the finished grade. You may want to add plants and ground covers to cascade over any border material and soften the edges—or to hide them completely.

In natural waterways, such as streams and creeks, the water's course can be enhanced through the use of undulating patterns. Sand and river pebbles, used in conjunction with boulders, are especially effective along the borders. Add some stepping stones so your visitors can cross the water, letting them further enjoy and become "part of" the landscape.

Opposite page: *The paving material of this reflecting pool reinforces its geometrical form. The lush foliage softens the geometric lines.* Above: *The soft, undulating border of this pond is enhanced by grass that extends to the water's edge.*

Equipment for Moving Water

Water is one of our most precious resources. We must not waste it, but conserve and appreciate it. A good design and the proper equipment will help you do both.

Pools and ponds with fountains, waterfalls, or waterways require electric **pumps** to circulate and recycle the water from the lowest point back up to the highest. There are two types of pumps available: the fully submersible pump, and the nonsubmersible pump. If your water is deep enough, you can use a submersible pump. A submersible pump operates quietly, needs no pump chamber or external piping, and never requires priming.

Nonsubmersible pumps are available in horizontal or vertical models. The horizontal pump is installed outside the pool; the vertical pump must be installed in shallow water and usually requires a spe-

cial compartment. There are pumps and fountain nozzles available for all situations. Choose your pump based on the anticipated volume of water, the height of the cascade above the water level of the pond, and the size of the spray.

Follow the manufacturer's directions carefully before installing and starting pumps. Electrical installations always should be approved by local codes and installed by trained electricians.

This water feature uses a pump to recycle the water from the pool for use in the fountain.

© Balthazar Korab

© Charles Mann

Your water feature should be kept brimming full. A **water-level-control device** keeps your feature full and acts in the same manner as a floatation device does in the tank of a toilet. Water pressure acting on the float keeps the valve closed. But if the water level drops, the pressure is no longer on the float and the valve opens, refilling the pool. This is especially advantageous in a pool with a submersible pump.

Water (especially moving water) will evaporate from the pool. To replace it you can either refill it from the garden hose, or let the level-control device refill it for you, reducing maintenance and possibly even preventing burnout of the pump.

Filter systems are often included as part of a pool or fountain. They prevent damage to the nozzle and pump, and reduce maintenance requirements.

If the water feature is connected to a potable water supply, you must be sure to install a **backflow prevention device**. This device is regulated by local plumbing codes, and it prevents accidental siphoning of the pool, pond, or waterway into the potable water system.

Overflow drains are used to maintain a constant water level during heavy rains or excessive filling. All pools, ponds, and waterways should be provided with a floor drain or other drainage device for cleaning and for draining during the win-

The equipment installed for your fountain must be able to pump water to the fall height. Also, the fall of the water should not splash or be blown by wind onto walkways, where there may be potential for slipping.

ter. Be sure your drain is connected to an approved drainage outlet.

Night lighting provides you with the ability to view your water feature twenty-four hours a day. It adds another dimension to your garden and is great for evening entertaining. Pool and pond lighting equipment is available in both 120-volt and 12-volt systems. The 12-volt system has the safety advantage of a lower shock hazard with the wattage flexibility of 120-volt fixtures. The maximum power for a 12-volt system is 300 watts. A 120-volt system can provide power in excess of 1,000 watts and the bulbs will last longer. The bulbs used for underwater lighting are not the same as those used above ground. Pool lights get hot and burn out if they are operated above water.

Night lighting, pumps, fountains, and aerators require electricity, so an electrical engineer should be retained. Keep in mind that it's possible a licensed electrician and plumber may be needed for any water feature you are going to install.

Maintenance

Quality materials, proper installation during construction, and adequate setup will produce a water feature that does not require a great amount of maintenance. Remember that your water feature will need some regular maintenance, including an occasional cleaning and routine checks to ensure that it is correctly filled with water.

Algae control

Probably the most aggravating maintenance problem with pools, ponds, and waterways is algae control. Without proper care, algae buildup can occur within a few short weeks. Many reflective pools and ponds are chemically treated to prevent algae and other unwanted aquatic growth through the use of one of the following: chlorination, bromination, ozonation, electrolytic sterilization, or Bacquacil treatment. The degree of treatment required depends on the weather, water temperature, and whether or not it is used for water play. Water treated with these products must not be allowed to contaminate a pool or pond that has any aquatic life.

Natural algae control is the best method for maintaining ponds and water gardens. A recirculating pump, air filter, and certain aquatic life can provide aeration and oxygenation, the best sources of algae control and water management.

© Charles Mann

PLANTS

Aquatic plants compete with the algae for nutrients found naturally in the water. Planting one submerged plant for every one to two feet (30 to 60 cm) of pond surface area is a good ratio to control algae. Water lilies are the most popular aquatic plants. They not only reduce algae maintenance, but also produce beautiful flowers, adding to the aesthetic quality of the pond. Remember that surface and surrounding plants need to be trimmed periodically.

FISH

Fish also enhance the beauty and enjoyment of a pond as well as reduce maintenance. They eat the algae and help to recirculate the water, reducing the need for oxygenation. However, a small pond with a large number of fish will probably require a filtering or recirculating system. The best balance of fish is one inch (25 mm) of fish length for every three to five gallons (13 to 23 l) of water.

A balance of plantings and aquatic life will provide a water feature that is relatively low in maintenance.

There are many fish available, including the famous Koi fish, used for centuries in Japanese aquatic gardens. Or choose comets, calicoes, or shubunkins. Fish should be fed every day, but not overfed. As long as the water is well oxygenated, the fish remain healthy. However, if you should notice one acting lethargic or with unusual swelling or blotches on its body, consult your local fish dealer for advice on how to treat it.

Other aquatic scavengers, such as snails, tadpoles, freshwater clams, and mussels, eat excess algae and control continued algae growth. Tadpoles and snails eat the larger hairy particles. Plants such as *Anacharis* will eat the dead algae.

The use of large-leaved varieties of plants adds color, contrast, and texture to this pond.

© Derek Fell

draining and cleaning

Many people believe that a well-balanced pool can go for years without having its water changed, but it is wise to change the water every spring. During the dry and hot weather of summer, if you see your fish coming to the surface to gasp for air, the oxygen levels in the water have dropped. Drain between one-half to two-thirds of the water and replace it with fresh water.

A yearly draining and cleaning is the easiest way to avoid possible trouble. It also is an opportunity to inspect the pool and to catch small hairline cracks before they become big ones.

If hairline cracks appear in a concrete or plastic pool, apply a coat or two of special pool sealer, caulking compound, epoxy, or use (in a concrete pool) a loose mixture of one part cement to three parts sand.

Repairing a major crack in a concrete pool requires more serious work. Cracks are usually caused by uneven settling

© Derek Fell

As in many gardens, trees and shrubs are essential elements to the beauty of the setting. It is important to clean up fallen leaves and prune aquatic plants to continue a balanced water environment.

(due to soft or filled ground) or by the expansion of ice in the winter. Drain the pool, then chisel the crack to a "V" shape. Fill in the hole with a caulking compound or a mixture of half cement and half sand (it must be wet enough to make it workable). Smooth the fill over and let it dry thoroughly. Remember, after repairing pool walls or floors, the pool must be cured again before restocking it with fish and plants.

Pools and ponds located in mild winter climates need very little care during the winter. Removing fallen leaves and other debris periodically will help lower the incidence of disease in the pool and will help improve its appearance. Also, an ugly buildup of debris on the bottom of the pool will cause the water to become thick, black, and smelly (this is more likely to occur during the summer months), due to decomposition of the debris.

This Japanese Garden at the Washington Park Arboretum in Seattle, Washington, is an example of a naturally balanced pond.

Large, natural ponds and those water features with moving water typically can keep themselves clean. A balanced and properly cared-for pool or pond will have a slightly greenish cast that occurs when the plants, fish, and algae all work together.

If you live in an area that suffers extreme winters, be sure to drain your pool before the freezing weather comes. Pools deeper than twenty-four inches (60 cm), however, are less likely to freeze completely. And moving water, such as a waterfall or fountain, will help to prevent surface ice—providing the pumps and pipes don't freeze.

Fish will not need feeding during the winter months. They will feed off the natural food in the water, and live off their own body fat, built up during the summer months. Rocks, deep water, and ledges can provide cover for fish and give them places to hibernate. In areas where shallow water will freeze, the fish should be brought indoors. Or place an electric immersion heater in the pool to keep the water from freezing.

Maintenance required for pools, ponds, and waterways takes less time if tended to on a regular basis. An algae-free pond is more aesthetically pleasing, and healthier for plants and aquatic life. The efforts you make toward the maintenance of your water feature will reward you with a unique garden element that will attract the attention of all.

The lilies incorporated into the formal pool of the Blake House Garden in California are planted to cover only a portion of the water surface.

© Derek Fell

chapter two

Design Considerations

Below: *Frank Lloyd Wright's design of the residence, Falling Water, in Bear Run, Pennsylvania, is a wonderful marriage of architecture and landscape.* Opposite page: *This lovely pool setting is enhanced by a soft fall of water that is slightly elevated above the paving level, nestled among planting pockets and trees.*

roperly designed pools, ponds, and waterways convey a rich sense of peace, nature, and harmony in the garden, and create a soothing, almost therapeutic atmosphere. When the feature suits your way of life, is positioned in the garden to enhance its beauty, and is proportionate in size to the garden environment, it creates a balance that gives a feeling of oneness with nature.

In most cases, we do not have the opportunity to begin the design of this environment with a blank palette. Usually, a home already exists and the property, with its surroundings, has already established a character and style. These existing conditions—both aesthetic and functional—should be incorporated into the design, since this water feature will become a permanent fixture within the property. To compose your water area, draw sketches of the proposed feature on a landscape plan, and study the site and the relationship of the elements to the whole environment. (Do this with a landscape architect or garden designer, if you are using one.)

Selecting the Setting

Water features are available in a wide range of sizes and materials, enabling most any property to blend water taste-

© Derek Fell

fully into the setting. To determine the most appropriate feature for your setting, study the immediate site and its relationship to the total scene around it. You can then determine the type of water feature that will integrate most successfully into the garden. Work with the land and its existing character and elements. The result you achieve will be an outdoor space that successfully merges manufactured parts with nature, that pleases the mind as much as the body.

A reflecting pool or pond fits in well with a level setting that enables the water to be still. Elements surrounding the water, such as ferns, trees, or sculpture, provide the vertical accents and shadows that will reflect onto the water. (Vertical elements are not crucial to an attractive reflection, however.) The reflection of the blue sky, moving clouds, birds in flight, or changes in light provide wonderful interest and variety.

A pool of still water may be raised and presented as a reservoir. Picture an eighteen-inch (45-cm) or waist-high wall that

© Nancy Hill

can be sat upon, bringing the water near the eye and close enough to touch.

A channel of water may also be placed in a flat setting, such as a courtyard. The source of the flow may be from a raised pool of gurgling water or a wall fountain that gently expresses water from a lion's mouth into a bowl, then spills over into the channel. As the water moves further away from the source, it becomes less active, more reflective. These features add vertical interest to an otherwise flat garden. They also provide dimension and relief to a monotonous scene or domineering wall.

If the garden setting offers changes in elevation, exaggerate these differences and create a waterway of moving water traveling to a pool or pond. As water automatically spills downward with gravity, make a waterway part of the natural topography, letting it end in a low part of the garden.

For a formal waterway, the water source may be from a pool or spout that spills through a series of geometrical res-

Providing a view of only a portion of a water feature makes one curious to follow a path to see what else it has to offer.

ervoirs or steps, ending in a pool adjacent to a paved patio or garden room.

The source of the water for a natural-looking stream or waterfall may be a small pond or grotto located near a high point of the garden. The water source may be hidden by plants and rocks. Or perhaps the water appears as though it began from around the corner or behind a

bermed area, from where it meanders into an informal pond in a low point of the garden.

Informal ponds of irregular shape must appear as though they have always been a part of the garden. They should have a backdrop of lush evergreens and a border of waterside plantings complemented with indigenous rocks or stones.

© Lynn Karlin

formal or informal

Try to design a water feature that will be a sincere part of your setting. All garden water features can be divided into two categories: formal or informal. *Formal* water features include all pools of regular shape, all fountains, and any water in a situation where it clearly could not have arrived by itself. *Informal* includes any-thing that appears natural. Informal set-tings are designed and installed so well that they actually appear to be part of nature's original design.

One interesting informal design com-bines a natural-looking waterfall with an existing oval swimming pool. The prop-erty is large with gentle-grade changes that increase behind the pool area. Large trees on the property further enhance the "natural" setting. The water source appears to be descending from a creek bed planted with lush grasses. (In reality, the creek bed was dry.) The water actu-ally originates in a small manufactured pond at the base of the dry creek. A

By camouflaging man-made materials with rocks and plants, this pond appears very natural.

bridge located within this area helps to camouflage the transition. The water then spills over rocks and into the pool. To further enhance the setting, waterside plantings border the pond and are located in pockets along the pool. A few large boulders have been set into the pool bond beam to replace the diving board and provide relief from the precast concrete coping. The success of this design can be attributed to its camouflage of the artificial water source and its blending naturally into the existing environment.

What if you want a "natural" style in a small, flat backyard? By using the principles of Japanese garden design, you can create a miniature landscape that appears natural, in a more subtle way. This design utilizes a spring and an outcrop of rock in a small backyard garden. By admitting this unlikeliness and using good garden-design principles, a beautiful setting can be created within what was once a previously nondescript scene, transforming the garden into a sculptural work of art.

Locating and Positioning the Feature

A traditional pool, natural pond, or moving waterway will add dramatic, unique qualities to the garden and will become the primary focal point.

Selecting the most suitable location for a water feature within your garden is very important. The best placement is where it will provide you the most pleasure, kept close enough to be seen and heard and to be enjoyed for its beauty. If the feature is located along a path or away from the house, provide seating near the water so the viewer can relax while in the garden.

Small accents

Small bowls and containers are popular water accents because they are easy to install, are available in a range of sizes and materials, are quite affordable, and may be moved, if they are lightweight. Their placement in the garden greatly affects their effectiveness.

Left: *One should be able to sit and relax within the garden as well as walk around it to experience all it has to offer.* Above: *A birdbath located along a path offers ornamentation as well as refreshment for wildlife.*

A small water accent should be located near a patio, on wide steps, or along a walkway or path, rather than out in the garden where its beauty may be unnoticed. Create a charming garden ornament by placing a small, movable water accent above ground level on a bench, low wall, wide steps, or table.

If a small pool is sunk in the ground, frame it with lush plantings to give a larger and more established appearance.

A wall fountain can be used where space is limited to bring interest to an otherwise austere wall.

Locate a small formal pool adjacent to a terrace and unite the two elements by adding paving material around the edge of the pool. If a pool or fountain is to be located in the center of a patio or courtyard, include potted plants and perimeter planting areas to soften the area. Also, be sure there is sufficient space around the feature if the area is used for circulation or entertainment. (In this case, you may consider locating the feature to one side or nestling it into a corner.)

Swimming pools and spas

Adding a swimming pool to your garden must be done very carefully to create a cohesive environment. By its size and its proportion to the site, a swimming pool has the potential to dominate the landscape. On the other hand, a well-designed swimming pool can enhance even a small garden. Adding a pool to your garden can be done quite successfully if the form and position of the pool

© Charles Mann

The setting of this hot tub is comfortable, relaxing, and one that provides privacy to the user.

are in keeping with the natural topography, the shape of the site, and the surrounding area.

Determining the location and position of a swimming pool, spa, or hot tub must also include certain lifestyle consider-ations, such as convenience, privacy, protection from crosswinds, and space for sunning. These needs must be taken into consideration when designing the area to enable full use and enjoyment of these water and play environments.

Spa designs can be incorporated into almost any setting and style. Here a Japanese feel is created with the use of beautiful privacy screens.

If you are adding both a swimming pool and a spa, you may prefer to nestle the spa into the setting with rock and foliage or locate it at a higher elevation. This will provide a separation from the more "animated activities" that occur in a swimming pool.

You must consider the distance you are willing to travel from the house to the pool or tub, especially in chilly weather. It's great fun to sit outdoors in a hot spa, especially when it's snowing outside; but the journey outside is best when it is a short distance from the warm house.

© Derek Fell

The pool area should be conveniently located near kitchen facilities (for entertaining) and a changing area with showers. If there is enough room, a pool house may even be incorporated into the design. A pool house may also provide storage for garden furniture and pool equipment.

Consider a site that will provide privacy from neighbors and shelter from the wind. You may want to place the pool, spa, or hot tub in a location that does not permit views from outside locations. Or, include in the design a screen provided by a formal hedge, a dense planting of shrubbery, a fence, a wall, or a garden structure such as a gazebo.

These garden screens can also provide protection from crosswinds that may be a bother when using your water feature. The spray from a waterfall or fountain can be misdirected by strong winds, causing unwanted mist and greater evaporation of the water. Wind will also blow debris into the water. Consider the general direction from which the prevailing winds occur in the area and position the feature so that the winds do not prevent use of the feature or cause greater maintenance problems.

Your pool should be in an area that will provide space for sunning, lounge chairs, and entertainment. This may be an adjacent area of lawn, paving, or decking. Or, it may even be as simple as a large, comfortable bench.

When providing an outdoor space where people will be sitting and enjoying their surroundings (whether it be in the water or on a patio), be certain to take advantage not only of the elements and views within the garden setting, but also those beyond. If trees are located on an

This pool house is incorporated into the design of this fun and dynamic pool area.

The ornate design of the Longwood Gardens in Chester, Pennsylvania, incorporates extensive formal water features throughout the estate.

© Anita Sabarese

adjacent property, let them provide a backdrop to your setting. Or extend the scene to distant hills or city lights. Block out or distract from unattractive views, but take advantage of the world around you by bringing attention to its beauty.

Incorporating water features throughout your property

A property that is large or provides various nooks and crannies can include the excitement of placing a pool, pond, or waterway around a bend. Perhaps one is first attracted to the feature by the sound of water, or by following flowing lines of a garden path. Do not hide the feature so much that it is unnoticed.

A large or varying shaped property can contain numerous water features, such as a swimming pool, spa, stream, reflecting pond, or inner courtyard fountain, located about the site. Certain details or materials can be selected from the natural terrain, architectural style, or interior design and incorporated into each area to provide a planned continuity throughout the property. Wouldn't it be grand to carry a water theme throughout the property?

When selecting the location of the pool, pond, or waterway, certain technical aspects should be considered. These include the size and depth of the proposed feature, existing soil conditions, accessibility to the site, access to necessary utility connections, and the location of pool equipment.

If the feature requires excavation of a great amount of soil, access to the site for mechanical equipment is very important. Also, easy access is best for delivery of materials during construction.

Sandy and rocky soils are the most difficult to dig through, clay and loose soils the easiest. If the soil is very rocky or if there is a high water table, you may consider incorporating a raised pool as the water feature. Having utility connections for water and electricity near the feature is beneficial. If large equipment is necessary to operate a pool, pond, spa, waterfall, or fountain, consideration must be made for equipment location. Not only might this equipment be noisy, it is also unattractive. Locating it in a

© Lynn Karlin

garage or pool house is great. Also, masonry walls, camouflaged by vines and large shrubs, provide noise reduction and visual blockage.

If these technical considerations are a problem, you might consider an alternative location for your water feature,

This swimming pool has direct access to the house and entertainment area, making it an integral part of the setting.

Right: *A majority of the space available in this garden is used for the swimming pool and jacuzzi. The flowing lines, subtle level changes, and dark pool surface all contribute to a garden that is inviting and relaxing.* Opposite page: *The long, narrow form of this pool makes the garden appear longer than it actually is. The arch provides a focal point, and the irises provide a vertical accent in contrast to the horizontal lines of the pool.*

which may positively affect the cost of installation, construction time, convenience in your daily living, and enjoyment of the feature.

© Derek Fell

Size and Proportion

It is not necessary for a pool, pond, or waterway to be large in order for it to be effective. Rather, a feature should be proportionate to the existing setting and the environment being created. The elements of the setting must be proportional to each other and similar enough to create a flowing transition, yet different enough to provide attractive contrast with each other. The size of the feature should be affordable, as large or as small as the site can accommodate, and sufficient to provide the functions you want.

Water offers complete flexibility to suit any setting and can visually alter the size and shape of a site. To make the most of a small area, the light-reflecting qualities of water will add an extra dimension and be a great asset to the garden. A wide pool positioned horizontally across a long garden will make the garden appear shorter. A long, thin pool or stream placed the length of the garden will make it appear longer. Visual tricks can be played with mirrors placed on a wall to expand the garden. A wooden deck can overlap the water's edge to give the impression that the water flows underneath. The presence of water in the garden, no matter how large or small, brings life and interest.

If the pool or pond is intended for aquatic life, it must be eighteen to twenty-four inches (45 to 60 cm) deep. This will allow a twelve-inch (30-cm) plant container to be immersed in the pool so that the soil surface is about eight to twelve inches (20 to 30 cm) underwater. The pool must provide enough depth for protection of plants and fish during winter cold and freezing. The appropriate depth will depend on the lowest temperature of the region and the frost line (call your local Department of Agriculture for this information).

Another size consideration is the quantity of plants and fish you want in the pool or pond. The size of the pool determines the size of the plants and the kinds of foliage to use. A single water lily will

© Charles Mann

No matter what scale you are working with, no one can argue the beauty a pond provides in a garden.

cover almost twelve square feet (1.1 sq.m) of surface area, whereas a dwarf lily requires about four square feet (0.4 sq.m) of surface area. Remember, too, that aquatic plants should not cover more than 50 percent of the surface area.

The depth of a pool or pond with a fountain or waterfall should be a minimum of eight inches (20 cm). If a submersible pump is located in the basin, there should be a minimum of two inches (5 cm) of water over the top of the pump.

A reflecting pool or pond need not be very deep: six inches (15 cm) of water with a dark surface is all of the water you will need for your pool to have excellent reflective qualities.

Pools and ponds with excessive depths may be considered swimming pools rather than purely ornamental features. Check with your local governing codes, which restrict maximum depths of ornamental water features. If the depth of the feature makes it a swimming pool, spa, or hot tub, you may need to take additional precautions, such as installing safety fencing, gates, and covers to protect you from certain liabilities.

Excessive pool and pond depths are potentially hazardous if children are nearby or will be using the pool area. By providing shallow depths at the edge and increased depths at the center, you provide a somewhat safer environment. (For more information on safeguarding your garden, see page 62.)

*b*asin size

Just as the size of a pool or pond must be in scale with its surroundings, a fountain or waterfall must be in scale with the size of the pool. The size of the fountain basin should provide for sufficient water surface to contain the splash from the falling water. This will prevent splashing of water onto patios or walkways.

When a water feature moves through a series of multilevel pools and upper-level basins, the lowest pool will have a reduction in the water level during operation. Once the pool is shut off, the circulating water volume will raise the water level of the lowest pool. A large bottom basin will provide the surface area necessary to store the water of the pools that empty into it when the system is shut off.

In designing the spill of water, certain edge treatments over which water falls can affect the appearance of the water. Smooth concrete or tile edges will spill water in a smooth sheet form. A natural waterfall of rock and boulders will create an irregular spill of water. An overhanging fall should provide a lip at the top of the waterfall so that the water does not trickle down the back of the wall or rocks.

Both the lines of this garden and the statuette draw the eye to this formal pool.

It is fun to play with water and experiment with the effects of moving it in different forms and over different textures. This is what makes the features so unique and interesting.

These stone stairways invite you down to the pool.

Safety

The aesthetic qualities and pleasures that a water feature can add to your living environment are limitless. However, there are risks that must be considered in having this beautiful feature as an element of your garden. In addition to the safety precautions required by local codes and manufacturers (such as electrical, plumbing, and prevention of accidental drowning in deep water), you should consider additional safety measures when designing your water environment.

If children will be in the area, especially those who are under five years old, pools of any depth are dangerous. You may want to wait to install your pool or pond until the children are older. Where you don't want an exposed stretch of water, it is safe to install a wall-mounted feature or a very shallow bubble fountain that drains into a concealed reservoir. A trickle of water over a pebbly surface is safe to play in, but adult supervision is always necessary.

© Derek Fell

This lovely garden intrigues those walking past and offers a resting place for anyone who would like to sit upon the ledge.

Night lighting will bring wonderful aesthetic highlighting to your garden and enable use of your garden in the evening. Any expanse of water should be lit at night to define its limits, especially where the water may be hidden by lush plantings. All paths, steps, and changes in elevation should also be well lit.

A safe outdoor environment provides you with the security of knowing that the area and all that is has to offer will bring pleasure to all who experience it.

It is an excellent idea to place nonslip paving material around and near the water to provide ease and safety for walking. Surfaces with a textured finish such as brick, broom-finished or exposed aggregate concrete, non-polished granite, or even a wood deck make wonderful and safe paving surfaces. Loose materials such as gravel, stone, and sand should only be used where there is little chance of someone stumbling or falling, and thereby injuring him or herself.

chapter three

Plants to Use
In and Around Your
Water Garden

t is the incorporation of plants that unites the water, its container, and the surrounding environment. The relationship between the vegetation, the water feature, the garden, and the site should be sufficient to establish the feature as part of the landscape. It should not, however, hide the beauty of the water. It is important to know where to place the appropriate plants, when enough is enough, and when no plants are needed at all.

A formal pool is a freestanding element in the garden. The water and the feature retaining it are the focal points, not the plants. Thus, any planting around the border should be used to bring attention to the water. Planting within the water, such as the sudden vertical of a reed or iris, will contrast beautifully with the horizontal form of the water. If a pool or pond is to mirror the surroundings, at least two-thirds of the water surface should be clear of aquatic plants. It is very

The lilies within this pool provide a lovely "base" for the garden statue.

important to the design and health of plants not to overplant.

An informal or natural pond or waterway must be planted as nature would have planted it. Depending upon the available moisture level throughout the year, the suitable periphery plants selected may vary from a moist meadow to a swamp environment. Be certain that the synthetic edges of a natural pond are camouflaged by plants and other natural materials.

The rate of flow in a stream or channel affects the form of the planting along its banks. The edge of a swiftly moving stretch of water is best treated simply, bringing focus and attention to the movement and sound of the water. A more serene area where the water collects should be developed with accent plants. Special water-loving plants will thrive at the edge of a stone-bordered woodland pool.

Pools and ponds with submersible plants require full sunlight for good growth. The periphery plantings must be sun tolerant, as well as provide a moisture-loving appearance.

In some instances, the water feature will be located in the shade, not permitting adequate sunlight for aquatic plants. In this case, use shade-tolerant plants.

The plants you choose for your water garden can add outstanding texture, contrast, color, and fragrance to the area. The bold form and texture of plants such as lotus, papyrus, rushes, grasses, and water lilies provide very dramatic effects. Varia-

This lovely stream, located in the gardens of Baldwin Manor in Maui, flows along the natural contours of the land, surrounded by plants that create a water-loving atmosphere.

© Derek Fell

tions in leaf size, shape, and color provide contrast. Fragrant, flowering plants provide additional sensory enjoyment. Choose your plants to enhance the character of the water feature, but bear in mind that too much variety will create chaos.

Background plantings can create a screen for privacy and separate the garden from the rest of the world. They create a backdrop to the stage being created. The plant varieties selected should be predominantly evergreens, placed in flowing groups to unify the garden.

Trees with weeping forms and interesting branching structures imitate spilling water and provide wonderful reflective patterns. Their foliage fluttering in the wind, reflecting color into the water, and possibly providing color changes with the seasons, will truly accent the edge of any water feature.

If you live where snow falls, take advantage of plants for their snow-catching ability, deciduous branching patterns, winter berries, large seedpods, golden

This pavillion is enhanced by the mirroring effects of the water, the horizontal form of the water lilies, and the vertical accents of the foliage that frame the view.

leaves, and spiky textures. Give these plantings an eye-catching spot.

Select plants and locate them for their year-round value in the garden. Consider

© Charles Mann

weather changes, and their degree of drought resistance.

Grow plants that are native to your area and that will acclimate well to the local soils and climate. Respect the natural ecology of the garden, but exploit its natural beauty. Place plants that have similar soil and sun requirements together. Observe the local terrain and take advice from a nearby nursery.

For the gardener, the opportunity to grow aquatic plants brings a special kind of satisfaction. There are no special tricks or secrets involved in the cultivation of water plants; they offer lovely, colorful blooms and unique foliage without a lot of care.

Following is a list of some of the numerous plants available for waterside or submerged use. Some species may be better adapted to your area than others. If there is a particular plant that you are interested in, but it is not available in or adaptable to your area, talk to the specialists at your local nursery or refer to the sources listed in the back of the book for help in select-

such qualities as spring blossoms and blossom color, growing characteristics, possible shadow patterns to be caught on water, walls, and paving, leaf response to

The Japanese Bridge of Monet's Garden is truly a balance of texture, shape, size, color, and contrast.

ing alternative plants that will thrive in your garden.

The plants are first listed by their botanical name, followed by their common name. Beneath this is the size of the plant's mature growth, height, or depth (if submerged), followed by the width of their mature growth. The following key applies:

First Line: Botanical Name, Common Name (or No Common Name, NCN), Hardiness Zone
Second Line: Height, Width
Third Line: Description

Waterside Plants

These are the marsh and bog plants; they include some beautiful species. The size, texture, and color of the foliage will enhance the water feature. Border plants will grow in any good heavy loam and need little attention. Placing them at their proper planting level is important. Some like their root crowns just slightly above water level; others must have roots in marshy soil. Several need six to ten inches (15 to 25 cm) of water above the crown of the plant. Many of these plants can be used in planting boxes, too.

Large-leaved varieties

These types of plants provide great texture and drama to your waterside garden. They require space and should not be used where they will dominate the setting. Rather, they should be used for accent.

Cardiocrinum giganteum, NCN, Z3

- Height 6 to 9 feet (1.8 to 2.7 m); Width 36 inches (.91 m)

- This is the largest flowering plant in the lily family, has a slightly tropical appearance, and looks particularly good planted in a group, the bold leaves creating an almost exotic effect. In summer it produces large, trumpet-shaped flowers and, later, large seedpods.

- A hardy plant, best in partial shade and planted in very deep (thirty-six inches [91 cm]) humus-enriched soil. Ensure good drainage around the bulbs to prevent rotting. The plant takes about six years to flower and dies after flowering.

Gunnera manicata, NCN, Z9

- Height 6 to 13 feet (1.8 to 3.9 m); Width 10 to 15 feet (3 to 4.5 m)

- A hardy perennial, it is the largest-leaved plant that can be grown under garden conditions. The leaves can be up to thirteen feet (3.9 m) across. It likes the deep mud at the side of a large pond or lake and does not mind shade.

- In cold climates, it should be covered during severe winter months; alternatively, cut off the leaves in autumn and wrap them over the crown of the plant.

© Derek Fell

Cardiocrinum giganteum.

***G. scabra*, NCN, Z9**

- Height 6 feet (1.8 m); Width 6 to 10 feet (1.8 to 3 m)

- This variety has slightly smaller leaves and tends to spread more than *G. manicata*. It is hardier, tolerating colder conditions. However, treat *G. scabra* in the same way, protecting it well against frosts and cold winds in winter.

***Hosta fortunei*, Plantain Lily, Z3**

- Height 24 inches (60 cm); Width 16 inches (40 cm)

- The deeply veined gray-green leaves give the plant its own character with blue-lilac flowers on erect spikes with small hanging bells in midsummer. Although it is rather susceptible to slugs, it is a valuable asset to the garden.

- It is happiest in damp, shady conditions in soil enriched with peat or humus.

- Other wonderful varieties to use are *H. sieboldiana* 'Elegans,' and *H. ventricosa*.

***Ligularia clivorum* 'Desdemona,' NCN, Z8**

- Height 4 feet (1.2 m); Width 3 feet (90 cm)

- This hardy hybrid has purple coloring on the underside of its large, heart-shaped leaves with large flowerheads, five feet (1.5 m) tall, carrying up to twenty orange, daisylike flowers in late summer. Attracts bees and butterflies.

- It is not fussy about soil type as long as the soil is moist and well-fed with humus. It needs shelter from strong sunlight and wind.

- Other common varieties are *L. dentata* 'Gregynog Gold,' *L. Przewalskii,* and *L. stenocephala* 'Rocket.'

© Derek Fell

Lysichiton americanum, Skunk Cabbage, Z7

- Height 4 feet (1.2 m); Width 24 inches (60 cm)

- This hardy herbaceous perennial thrives in sun in muddy and boggy situations where its roots can penetrate four to six feet (1.2 to 1.8 m) deep. Although slow to establish itself, it is a dramatic plant that sprouts large, bright yellow arumlike flowers in early spring, followed by giant banana-shaped leaves that appear out of the mud and grow to five feet (1.5 m). The flowers give off a strong scent, particularly on a warm day, giving the plant its common name.

Rheum palmatum, Rhubarb, Z4

- Height 6 feet (1.8 m); Width 6 feet (1.8 m)

- This ornamental rhubarb is an eye-catching and hardy perennial. It produces overlapping bright green leaves up to thirty-six inches (90 cm) across, and its flowers are borne in a panicle. It grows in sun or shade and likes a damp, compost-enriched soil with its roots out of water.

- The hybrid *R. p.* 'Purpureum' has a finer-cut leaf with red-purple undersides flowering with a tall pink flower in early summer. This plant is especially good for areas where a large leaf is needed to contrast the irises or primulas.

Lysichiton americanum *(Yellow Skunk Cabbage).*

Zantedeschia aethiopica, Arum Lily, Z7

- Height 36 inches (90 cm); Width 35 inches (88 cm)

- This lily can be grown both in the water (in wire baskets) or as a waterside plant. Its tropical appearance, with its spectacular white flowers, makes it ideal for city gardens.

- It is not suitable for very cold climates, does not tolerate frost, and should be lifted and kept in a frost-free greenhouse during winter. In warmer climates, it grows at the edge of ponds to provide continuous spring and summer flowering.

Small-leaved varieties

These plantings are less dramatic and can be used in masses in large pools or ponds. They provide wonderful flowering effects and can be used in small-sized water features. Most of the plants listed here will tolerate wet soil and some prefer their roots submerged in water. Due to their flowering abilities, most require a sunny location.

Calla palustris, Bog Arum, Z8

- Height 4 inches (10 cm); Width many feet (a few meters)

- This hardy plant anchors itself at the waterside and floats out over the surface, forming large mats of small, shiny, heart-shaped leaves with white arumlike flowers in early summer, or after the second year, in late spring. It is a good plant for bog gardens; it is impartial to soil but requires sun. A useful plant for softening the edges of ponds.

***Caltha palustris*, Marsh Marigold, Z2**

- Height 12 inches (30 cm); Width 12 inches (30 cm)

- This is a hardy plant, with heart-shaped leaves. It flowers early in spring and looks at its best when planted in large groups to accentuate the large yellow flowers. It prefers rich soil and sun.

- *C. p. pleno*, the double-flowered variety, is more compact and better suited to small urban ponds, where its leaves make a good ground cover. 'Alba' is a white form that prefers a slightly drier situation.

© Derek Fell

***Geum rivale*, Water Avens, Z4**

- Height 24 inches (60 cm); Width 20 inches (50 cm)

- A hardy spreading plant good for growing in damp soil, in sun or shade. Insignificant, soft orange flowers stand twelve inches (30 cm) above clusters of green, divided leaves on hairy, red stems.

- *G.* x *Borisii* makes a good ground cover, producing neat clumps of dark green leaves and bright orange-red flowers in early summer. It will also thrive well in a border but requires good mulching with well-rotted manure or compost. Geum is best planted in large groups to give maximum color impact, and they will also combine well with primulas and hostas.

Caltha palustris *(Marsh Marigold).*

Iris kaempferi, Japanese Iris, Z5

- Height 36 inches (90 cm); Width 18 inches (45 cm)

- Most species of iris are hardy and require little attention except being kept free of invasive plants and grasses. They have slender deciduous foliage and purple flowers in midsummer. The colors of its cultivars range from white through pink and lavender to violet. It likes a wet, rich soil and sun.

- Other beautiful irises to choose from are *I. laevigata* (Water Iris), *I. l.* 'Variegata,' and *I. pseudacorus* (Yellow Flag).

Iris kaempferi *(Japanese Iris)*.

Mentha aquatica, Water Mint, Z8

- Height 12 inches (30 cm); Width indefinite

- The hardy water mint thrives in shallow water. It will live either on the water surface or in soil and has bright green leaves in shady situations, turning to purple in full sunlight. It has a minty smell and flavor and produces spiky pom-poms of bright blue flowers in late summer. It can be invasive.

Pontederia cordata, Pickerel Weed, Z4

- Height 24 inches (60 cm); Width 6 inches (15 cm)

- Heart-shaped, waxy, light green leaves on long stalks, and attractive spikes of blue flowers in late summer. It looks good planted in mass to soften a pond edge.

Sagittaria japonica, Japanese Arrowhead, Z5

- Height 12 inches (30 cm); Width 8 inches (20 cm)

- This hardy plant has large, arrow-shaped leaves and beautiful, white double flowers up to two inches (5 cm) across. It should be planted in shallow water no deeper than five inches (13 cm).

- Another wonderful variety to use is *S. sagittifolia* (Common Arrowhead).

Moisture-Loving Plants

These plants require less water than the waterside plantings; however, they still prefer a moist, well-drained soil.

Astilbe x *arendsii*, NCN, Z4

- Height 2 to 5 feet (60 to 150 cm); Width 8 to 36 inches (20 to 90 cm)

- The astilbe family has many garden hybrids. They are invaluable plants for the gardener, since they are hardy and have a wide range of colors.

A. chinensis 'Pumila', NCN, Z4

- Height 24 inches (60 cm); Width 24 inches (60 cm)

- This is a low-growing form that is ideal for color in moist, shady places. It has beautiful spikes of rose-colored flowers in midsummer.

Hemerocallis, Day Lily, Z4

- Height 3 feet (90 cm); Width 3 feet (90 cm)

- These tough, prolific plants create beautiful grass-type borders on sunny edges of ponds and pools. The wide variety of flower colors available makes them a fun plant to use in masses.

Hosta fortunei 'Aurea', NCN, Z3

- Height 20 inches (50 cm); Width 20 inches (50 cm)

- This provides a hardy ground cover to the water's edge and is not too invasive. It will tolerate full sun if given plenty of moisture.

H. lancifolia, NCN, Z3

- Height 18 inches (45 cm); Width 12 to 24 inches (30 to 60 cm)

- This hosta has smaller, dark green leaves and can be used in much the same way. This variety requires some shade.

Iris sibirica, NCN, Z3

- Height 3 feet (90 cm); Width 3 feet (90 cm)

- This iris is a hardy plant for waterside planting, but will also tolerate drier conditions. It prefers sun and grows in clumps, spreading by seed. There are many different color varieties, blue and white being the most popular.

Polygonum distorta 'Superbum', Knotweed, Z4

- Height 16 inches (40 cm); Width indefinite

- This plant can be quite invasive, but is controllable. It is hardy, grows near water, and tolerates shade. It will grow in full sun if moisture is sufficient. It has long, tall leaves with mauve-pink flowers blooming in summer that look like small pokers.

Primula florindae, Himalayan Cowslip, Z5

- Height 3 feet (90 cm); Width 3 feet (90 cm)

- This tall primula has yellow flowers in midsummer and will grow right at the water's edge. The red-colored roots are effective when planted in clusters. All primulas grow well in acid-rich woodland soil in half shade. They are hardy as short-lived perennials.

- Other varieties of different size and color include *P. helodoxa*, *P. japonica*, and *P. pulverulenta*.

Ferns

Ferns are wonderful plants to use in shady locations. Their graceful forms make them lovely choices to border the water feature or create a backdrop when planted in mass. There are many ferns available.

Adiantum aethiopicum, Maidenhair Fern, Z8

* Height 24 inches (60 cm); Width 3 feet (90 cm)

* This is a tender fern that offers soft green foliage. It is also a good fern to grow in containers.

Dicksonia antarctica, Tree Fern, Z9

* Height to 20 feet (6 m); Width 6 to 10 foot canopy (1.8 to 3 m)

* This tree fern is semi-hardy with a brown trunk and bright green lacy fronds above. It can be grown in large containers, near water, or by an indoor water garden. It is only suitable for mild, frost-free climates.

Adiantum aethiopicum
(Maidenhair Fern).

Osmunda regalis, Royal Fern, Z3

* Height 5 feet (1.5 m); Width 5 feet (1.5 m)

* This is a hardy fern, ideal for boggy soil, that gives a lovely reflection. In autumn the leaves change color to orange, then copper. It enjoys a slightly shady spot where the roots can penetrate deep moist soil.

Phyllitis scolopendrium, Hart's Tongue Fern, Z6

* Height 14 inches (35 cm); Width 12 inches (30 cm)

* This hardy fern grows well in moist or dry conditions and is suited for banks and rocky stream edges. The bright green fronds will soften edges and provide a natural look.

Equisetum hyemale
(Horsetail).

Reeds and Rushes

All reeds and rushes grow best with their roots in the water. They provide wonderful vertical accents and reflecting beauty in the water. Select those with the shape and growth habit that suits the design and the size of your feature. They generally are very invasive and should be contained in submerged buckets or wire baskets.

Acorus calamus variegatus, Sweet Flag, Z7

- Height 3 feet (90 cm); Width 12 inches (30 cm)

- This hardy plant has attractive green and cream striped leaves that are sweetly fragrant when crushed. It requires only a few inches of shallow water.

- Other smaller growing forms are *A. gramineus*, ten inches (25 cm) tall with finer leaves and solid green foliage. The very small *A. g.* 'Pusillus' is two to three inches (5 to 7 cm) tall and is not hardy.

Butomus umbellatus, Flowering Rush, Z5

- Height 3 feet (90 cm); Width 24 inches (60 cm)

- This hardy rush thrives in four-inch (10 cm) deep water in a sunny location. Its long, thin, sword-shaped leaves range from purple to green. The blossom in midsummer produces a head of many flowers resembling an upside down umbrella.

Equisetum hyemale, Horsetail, Z4

- Height 3 feet (90 cm); Width 12 inches (30 cm)

- This plant likes about one to four inches (25 to 100 mm) of water. It is one of the most popular pool plants, with tall, segmented leaves of apple-green color. It provides a striking vertical accent.

Juncus effusus 'Spiralis', Corkscrew Rush, Z3

- Height 13 to 16 feet (3.9 to 4.8 m); Width 3 feet (0.9 m)
- Many members of this species are too vigorous to grow in the garden, but this one, which is not so prolific, is worth growing for its stems, which look like corkscrews. This hardy plant will grow at the waterside in moist soil and will tolerate shade.

Scirpus lacustris, Common Bulrush, Z8

- Height 8 feet (2.4 m); Width 3 feet (0.9 m)
- This is the classic water-edge rush with its tall green stems and fat, brown, pokerlike heads, providing perfect cover for wildfowl. It is too tall and prolific for small water gardens. It is hardy and likes sun.
- Variegated varieties include *S. l.* 'Zebrinus,' *S. l.* 'Pictus,' and *S. l.* 'Albescens.'

S. tabernaemontani zebrinus, Zebra Rush, Z8

- Height 4 feet (120 cm); Width 24 inches (60 cm)
- This hardy rush has unusual cream and white horizontal markings on its variegated stem. Solid green stems should be removed. It favors shallow water and a sunny location.

Typha latifolia, Reed-mace or False Bulrush, Z8

- Height 6 to 8 feet (1.8 to 2.4 m); Width 3 feet (0.9 m)
- This is a familiar pond-edge plant with gray-green spiky leaves and tall brown pokers. It is good for the edges of large lakes.
- Variety *T. minima* is better-suited to small gardens with a height of only thirty inches (75 cm).

Grasses and Sedges

There are many varieties of attractive grasses and sedges that grow well at the water's edge. Their roots bind the soil at the edge of streams and ponds, and their form provides a soft vertical accent.

Arundo donax, Giant Reed, Z4

- Height 8 to 16 feet (2.4 to 4.8 m); Width 10 to 13 feet (3 to 3.9 m)
- This dramatic semi-hardy plant has tall, thick stems topped by long, blue-gray leaves. It likes damp, sandy soils in sunny locations. It may need protection around its base in cold winters.

Cyperus alternifolius, Umbrella Grass, Z8

- Height 3 feet (90 cm); Width 3 feet (90 cm)
- This is a highly decorative sedge that grows in a sunny location in shallow water or along the bank. The tall graceful stems are topped with a fine "umbrella" of slender leaves. It offers a striking contrast with large, broad-leaved waterside plants.

C. longus, Sweet Galingale, Z8

- Height 4 feet (120 cm); Width 3 feet (90 cm)
- This semi-hardy sedge produces tall, arched, slender dark green stems with drooping clusters of red-brown flowers. It enjoys sun and moisture and is useful for binding the banks of large ponds. Growing it in very dry locations will restrict its growth.

C. papyrus, Nile Grass, Papyrus, Z8

- Height 8 feet (2.4 m); Width 10 to 13 feet (3 to 3.9 m)
- This subtropical, tender sedge can be grown in a pot by an indoor water feature or outdoors in warmer areas. The foliage contrasts the water.

Spartina pectinata, Prairie Cordgrass, Z8

- Height 6 feet (1.8 m); Width 3 feet (0.9 m)
- This hardy grass grows in marshy locations. It prefers sun and makes a good show in large gardens, being too invasive for smaller ones.

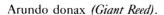

Arundo donax *(Giant Reed)*.

© Derek Fell

Floating and Submerged Aquatic Plants

Water lilies

These are the first plants that come to mind when one thinks of a water garden. There are hundreds of varieties of water lilies, the most hardy, colorful, and well-known belong to the genus *Nymphaea*. They can be divided into two classes: the hardy lilies, with medium to large-sized flowers; and the exotic tropicals, with larger and more colorful flowers. Almost all tropical lilies are fragrant; some open by day and others at night. Tropical water lilies are treated as annuals that die when winter comes; therefore, they will grow in all zones.

Once planted in a rich soil and sunny location, lilies require little care. Water lilies are best planted in wire baskets for easier maintenance. Hardy lilies can rest in their containers at the bottom of the pool through winter; below the frost line

© Wolfgang Kaehler

Pink Hardy Lily.

they will safely survive. If the frost line is below twenty-four inches (60 cm), place boards over the pool, with leaves on top for further insulation. To winter indoors, take hardies from the containers, wash them, store in clean, barely moist sand, and place in containers or bags with air holes.

The following are just a few of the varieties available.

Lilies add a splash of color to this dark-surfaced pool.

© Charles Mann

WHITE VARIETIES:

Albatross.
A snow-white lily; large and beautiful.

Gladstone.
Pure white, cup-shaped flowers; very large.

White Laydekeri.
Snow-white with yellow center; dwarf lily. Excellent bloomer.

Odorata.
Scented white flower; leaves with red undersides.

Pygmaea alba.
Dwarf, white flowers for small ponds and tubs.

PINK VARIETIES:

Laydekeri pupurata.
Rose-colored with purple tones.

Formosa.
A true pink and a terrific bloomer.

Helen Flower.
Light pink; fragrant; flowers well above water.

Mme. Wilfron Gonners.
Attractive double pink flower.

Neptune.
Pink blossoms and garnet stems.

RED VARIETIES:

Ellisiana.
Striking red flowers with dark red centers.

Laydederi fulgens.
Purplish red flower; excellent bloomer.

Newton.
Almost vermilion; large star-shaped flowers.

Sultan.
Large cherry-red lily; outer petals light rose; good bloomer; exquisite.

YELLOW VARIETIES:

Chromatella.
Pale yellow flowers; brown and green mottled leaves.

Mexican.
A little beauty from Mexico; can be a pest.

Pygmaea helvola.
Small yellow flowers that float on surface.

Sunrise.
canary-yellow blossoms, curved petals; magnificent.

© Charles Mann

The following are not water lilies, but are wonderful flowering water plants worth listing:

Aponogeton distachyus, **Water Hawthorn, Z10**

- Depth 3 feet (90 cm); Width several yards (meters)

- It has small, scented, white flowers and a tuberous rootstalk with floating narrow leaves.

Nelumbo **species, Lotus, zone varies**

- Depth 24 inches (60 cm); Width varies

- These incredible plants command interest and admiration because their beautiful large flowers, ranging in color from white to pink, red, and yellow, are truly spectacular. Ornamental woody fruits with perforations like a salt shaker are useful in dried arrangements. Lotus roots don't like corners, but do well in a round pot or tub. In winter, protect from freezing by covering the pool or storing the roots.

Red Hardy Lily.

floating and oxygenating plants

Floating and oxygenating plants are those that are not rooted. Some are surface-floating while others are completely or partly submerged. They spread rapidly, so thin them out every autumn. They should not be allowed to take up more than one third of the pool's volume. Rooted plants can be planted in wire baskets to control them more easily. Propagation is by division, and plants can be introduced by weighing the stems and dropping them to the pool bottom.

Eichhornia crassipes, Water Hyacinth, Z8

- Height (above water) 8 inches (20 cm); Width indefinite

- This beautiful tender plant thrives in tropical and subtropical climates. The flowers are spikes of mauve-blue with a touch of yellow. In cool climates, the plant may be floated in an inside tank with a layer of soil and slightly warmed water.

Elodea canadensis, Canadian Pondweed, Z3

- Depth 12 to 36 inches (30 to 90 cm); Width indefinite

- A free-floating plant with numerous tiny, attractive, dark green leaves. It is good for fish food and for spawning.

Hottonia palustris, Water Violet

- Depth 3 feet (90 cm); Width 20 inches (50 cm)

- Charming plant with loose spikes of mauve flowers. Leaves are submerged; flowers produced on leafless stems above water in early summer. Place in shallow water.

Lemna minor, Common Duckweed, Z4

- Depth shallow or deep water; Width indefinite

- A familiar sight in wild ponds and ditches, duckweed, another free-floating plant, is a favorite with garden fish. A hardy annual, it produces a mass of tiny green disks on long stems.

L. trisulca, Star Duckweed, Z4

- Depth shallow or deep water; Width indefinite

- A less-prolific variety, with oval, transparent green fronds and thin strands. It is an excellent purifier.

Myriophyllum spicatum, Milfoil, Z10

- Depth 3 feet (90 cm); Width indefinite

- A rooted perennial plant with attractive red, branched stems and olive-colored leaves. It produces tiny, red and yellow flowers and is an excellent purifier.

Pistoia stratiotes, Water Lettuce, Z8

- Depth shallow water; Width indefinite

- A short-lived tender perennial, water lettuce is a good foliage plant for the water surface. It does particularly well at water temperatures above sixty-eight degrees Fahrenheit (20°C). It resembles garden lettuce, making a pretty addition to any garden setting.

Trapa natans, Water Chestnut, Z5

- Depth shallow water; Width indefinite

- This hardy annual produces trailing stems with bronze and green floating leaves, looking slightly like holly, on swollen stalks. The large, black, spiny seeds resemble a large horse chestnut and are delicious to eat, either raw or roasted. However, they rarely ripen or set seed in temperate climates, where the summers are not warm enough.

Utricularia vulgaris, Bladderwort, Z3

- Depth 3 feet (90 cm); Width indefinite

- This hardy carnivorous plant produces feathery floating leaves with tiny bladderlike structures that catch small creatures such as daphnia. It also produces tiny, yellow, snapdragon-like flowers on stems above the water's surface.

Pistoia stratiotes *(Water Lettuce)*.

Rhododendron *(Azalea)*.

Shrubs

Shrubbery used around or adjacent to a pool, pond, or waterway can provide accent, color, border, and special interest. Shrubs should be allowed to grow in their natural habit, not well-manicured, to enhance the water effect. The following is a short listing of shrubs of particular interest that grow happily at the water's edge.

Cornus alba 'Sibirica', Siberian Dogwood, Z2

- Height 5 to 8 feet (1.5 to 2.4 m); Width 6 to 8 feet (1.8 to 2.4 m)

- The dogwoods are attractive, hardy, and deciduous shrubs, generally grown for their fine foliage and brightly colored bark in winter. All types will thrive in sun or light shade.

- Other varieties, growing in varying sizes are: *C. controversa* (Table Dogwood), *C. florida* (Flowering Dogwood), *C. kousa*, *C. nuttallii* (Mountain Dogwood), and *C. stolonifera* (American Dogwood).

© Wolfgang Kaehler

Phormium cookianum, Mountain Flax, Z8

- Height 3 feet (0.9 m); Width 4 to 5 feet (1.2 to 1.5 m)

- This half-hardy spreading plant is ideal for smaller water gardens as a background for lower water plants. It has widespread stems with green and orange tubular flowers. The seed heads are very decorative. It needs protection from cold winds and should be screened from northeast winds and from frosts. It will grow in different soil types and is happiest when close to water in full sun.

P. tenax, New Zealand Flax, Z8

- Height 5 to 8 feet (1.5 to 2.4 m); Width 6 feet (1.8 m)

- This plant makes an unusual feature in a large water garden with its stiff form and flower spikes carrying clusters of dull red flowers that become black bunches of short banana-shaped seedpods.

- Two cultivars are 'Purpureum' and 'Variegatum.'

Phyllostachys aureosulcata, Yellow-groove Bamboo, Z5

- Height 13 to 16 feet (3.9 to 4.8 m); Width 16 feet (4.8 m)

- This bamboo is used in Japanese gardens to emphasize or contrast with stone groupings near water or dry streams, or as a feature plant in a small patio area.

- Another wonderful variety of this species is *P. nigra* (Black Bamboo).

Rhododendron, Azalea, Z6

- Height 4 to 8 feet (1.2 to 2.4 m); Width 4 to 6 feet (1.2 to 1.8 m)

- Japanese varieties are evergreen, others are deciduous. They are of medium height, which makes them ideal for most garden settings. All azaleas prefer a moist, humus-rich, acid soil and part shade. There is a wide choice of flower colors ranging from white to bright red and purple.

Sorbaria aitchisonii, False Spiraea, Z4

- Height 8 to 10 feet (2.4 to 3 m); Width 10 to 13 feet (3 to 3.9 m)

- This hardy and deciduous shrub has elegant, feathery leaves on red stems and an attractive, bushy habit. In late summer it produces creamy white plumes of flowers. It prefers a moist peaty soil in full sun or light shade.

Trees

Every garden should have trees and the following are some examples of those that do well within a water garden setting.

Acer japonicum; *A. palmatum*, Japanese Maple, Z3

- Height 10 to 20 feet (3 to 6 m); Width 10 to 20 feet (3 to 6 m)

- These trees provide red and gold leaves in autumn and have many cultivars. Their branching patterns and single- or multitrunk forms look wonderful adjacent to pools, ponds, and waterways when foliated or deciduous. Planted in groups of odd numbers, the trees offer beauty for a grove-type setting.

- Other varieties to consider are *A. griseum* (Paperbark Maple), *A. j.* 'Aureum,' *A. j.* 'Aconitifolium,' *A. negundo* (Ash-leaved Maple or Box Elder), *A. n.* 'Variegatum,' and *A. p.* 'Dissectum.'

Acer *species (Maple).*

Betula occidentalis, Water Birch, Z4

- Height 20 to 25 feet (6 to 7.5 m); Width 10 feet (3 m)

- This birch produces dark green leaves and shiny, very dark brown bark. Like all birches, it is deciduous and hardy. Birch trees are lovely planted singly, but also are great planted as a multitrunk tree or in groups of odd numbers (three or more).

- Other varieties are available that offer weeping forms, white bark, and lovely growing habits. These are *B. papyrifera* (Canoe or Paperbark Birch) and *B. pendula* (European White Birch).

Salix babylonica 'Aurea', Golden
Weeping Willow, Z4

- Height 65 feet (19.5 m); Width 10 to 13 feet (3 to 3.9 m)

- The hardy, deciduous weeping willows with their drooping graceful branches of narrow leaves have long been familiar waterside trees. The golden color of this willow makes it popular. Full sun is required. Warning: Willows have invasive roots and should not be planted near the house or patio, where the foundation and paving could be damaged or water pipes disturbed.

- Other attractive willows of varying forms and sizes are: *S. fragilis* (Crack Willow) and *S. matsudana* 'Tortuosa' (Corkscrew Willow).

Salix *species (Willow).*

Taxodium distichum, **Swamp or Bald Cypress, Z5**

- Height 100 feet (30 m); Width 10 feet (3 m)

- This hardy, slow-growing, deciduous conifer has small, moss-green, frondlike leaves that turn a rich brown in autumn with tassels of yellow flowers. It prefers to be in a sunny position near water, where its roots show above the waterline.

Hardiness Zone Map

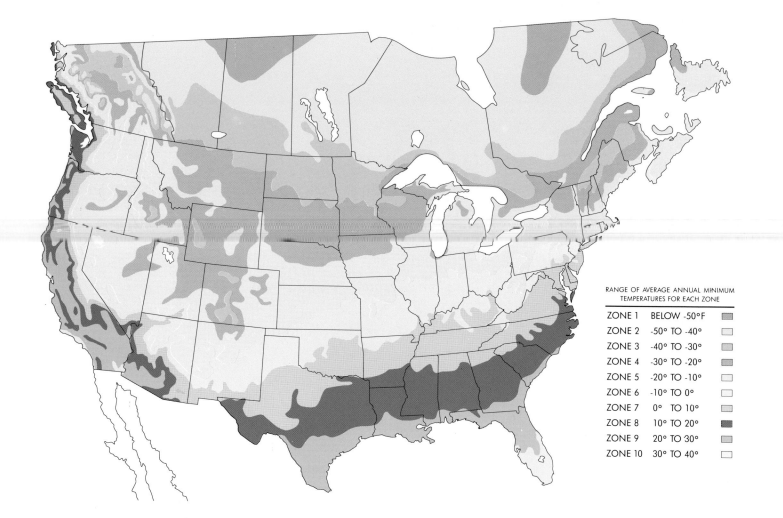

RANGE OF AVERAGE ANNUAL MINIMUM
TEMPERATURES FOR EACH ZONE

ZONE 1	BELOW -50°F	
ZONE 2	-50° TO -40°	
ZONE 3	-40° TO -30°	
ZONE 4	-30° TO -20°	
ZONE 5	-20° TO -10°	
ZONE 6	-10° TO 0°	
ZONE 7	0° TO 10°	
ZONE 8	10° TO 20°	
ZONE 9	20° TO 30°	
ZONE 10	30° TO 40°	

Sources

Dura Art Stone
P.O. Box 666
Fontana, CA 92334
• *Fountains*

EPI—Environmental Protection, Inc.
111 West Park Dr.
Kalkaska, MI 49646
• *Pond liners*

Florentine Craftsmen
46-24 28th St., Box LA
Long Island City, NY 11101

Green Thumb Nursery and Growers
5851 Myrtle Ave.
Eureka, CA 95501
• *Habitat restoration—wetlands*

Hermitage Gardens
P.O. Box 361
Route 5
West of Canastota, NY 13032
• *Fiberglass garden pools*

Kester's Wild Game Food Nurseries, Inc.
P.O. Box 516
Omro, WI 54963

Lilyponds Water Gardens
Dept. 2999   Dept. 2999
P.O. Box 10   P.O. Box 188
Buckeytown, MD   Brookshire, TX
21717-0010   77423-0188
• *Water gardening materials and information*

Loran Incorporated
1705 E. Colton Ave.
Redlands, CA 92373
• *Nightscaping—nightlighting*

Macaire
15010 Ventura Blvd., Suite 322
Sherman Oaks, CA 91403
• *Synthetic rock formations*

Revere Plastics
16 Industrial Ave.
Little Ferry, NJ 07643
• *Pond liners*

Schnoor's Aquatic Gardens & Koi Co.
P.O. Box 57
Jobstown, NJ 08041

SCS Company
5508 Pacifica Dr.
La Jolla, CA 92037
• *Participatory water play systems*

Slocum Water Gardens
Dept. LD9109
1101 Cypress Gardens Rd.
Winter Haven, FL 33880

Bibliography

Aurand, C. Douglas. *Fountains and Pools.* Mesa, Arizona: PDA Publishers Corporation, 1986.

Church, Thomas. *Your Private World.* San Francisco: Chronicle Books, 1969.

Cooper, Guy, Gordon Taylor and Clive Boursnell, forward by Sir Geoffrey Jellicoe. *English Water Gardens.* Boston and Toronto: Little, Brown and Company, 1987.

Douglas, Williams Lake, Susan R. Frey, Norman K. Johnson, Susan Littlefield and Michael Van Valkenburgh. *Garden Design.* New York: Simon & Schuster, 1984.

Fell, Derek, Dr. Darrell Apps, Dr. Fred Galle, Elizabeth Murray, Joan Pierson and Susan Roth. *The Complete Garden Planning Manual.* Los Angeles: HP Books, 1989.

Howland, Joseph E. *The House Beautiful Book of Gardens & Outdoor Living.* New York: Doubleday and Company, Inc, 1958.

Karson, Robin. *Fletcher Steele, Landscape Architect.* New York: Harry N. Abrams, Inc./Saga Press, Inc., 1989.

Landphair, Harlow C., and Fred Klatt, Jr. *Landscape Architecture Construction.* New York: Elsevier North Holland, Inc., 1979.

Newton, Norman T. *Design on the Land.* Cambridge: Belkhap Press of Harvard University, 1971.

Paul, Anthony, and Yvonne Rees. *The Water Garden.* New York and Markham, Ontario: Penguin Books, 1986.

Index